AMULET
KAZU KIBUISHI

BOOK TWO
THE STONEKEEPER'S CURSE

AN IMPRINT OF
SCHOLASTIC

NEW YORK   TORONTO   LONDON   AUCKLAND   SYDNEY   MEXICO CITY   NEW DELHI   HONG KONG   BUENOS AIRES

ISBN-978-93-89823-92-9

Edited by Sheila Keenan
Creative Director: David Saylor
Book Design by Phil Falco and Kazu Kibuishi

First edition: September 2009
This edition: November 2022

Printed in India

THAT WAS DONE ON THE KING'S ORDERS.

THE NEXT TIME I'M GOING TO BREAK SOMETHING.

GOT IT?

WHO GOES THERE?

PRINCE TRELLIS IS HERE TO SEE HIS FATHER, THE ELF KING.

AH, WELCOME BACK, SIR.

SHOVE!

OOF!

SHK!

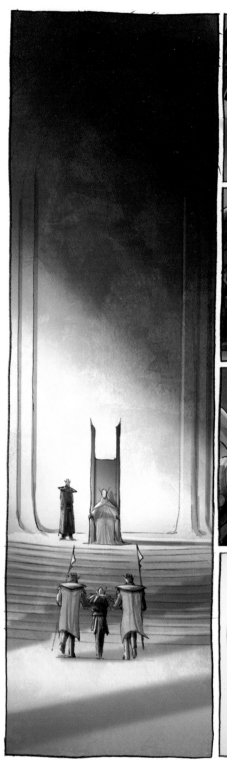

I GUESS IT SHOULD COME AS NO SURPRISE --

-- TO SEE THAT MY SON HAS FAILED ME AGAIN.

7

THERE. THAT SHOULD DO IT, NAVIN.

PSSSHT!

HOW'S IT GOING OVER THERE?

I GOT IT SECURED, COGSLEY.

GOOD WORK, KID. NOW LET'S GET THIS THING MOVING.

YOU TAKE THE DRIVER'S SEAT AND I'LL SHOW YOU HOW TO PILOT THE HOUSE.

REALLY?

IF FOR SOME REASON I'M DISABLED, THEN I EXPECT YOU TO TAKE THE CONTROLS.

YOU'RE MY INSURANCE POLICY, GOT IT?

GOT IT.

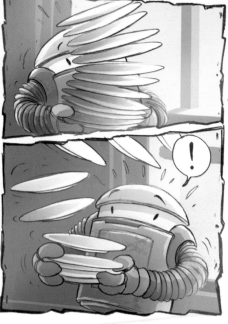

I HOPE EVERYONE LIKES THEIR EGGS SCRAMBLED.

THEODORE -- TAKE THIS TO CAPTAIN EMILY.

AND TELL HER WE'LL BE ARRIVING IN KANALIS SHORTLY.

YES, SIR.

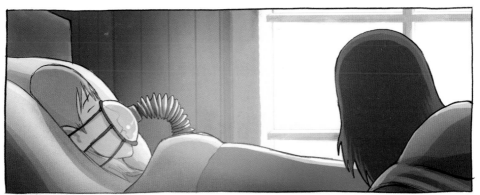

KLAK!

WE WILL BE ARRIVING IN KANALIS SOON.

THANK YOU, THEODORE.

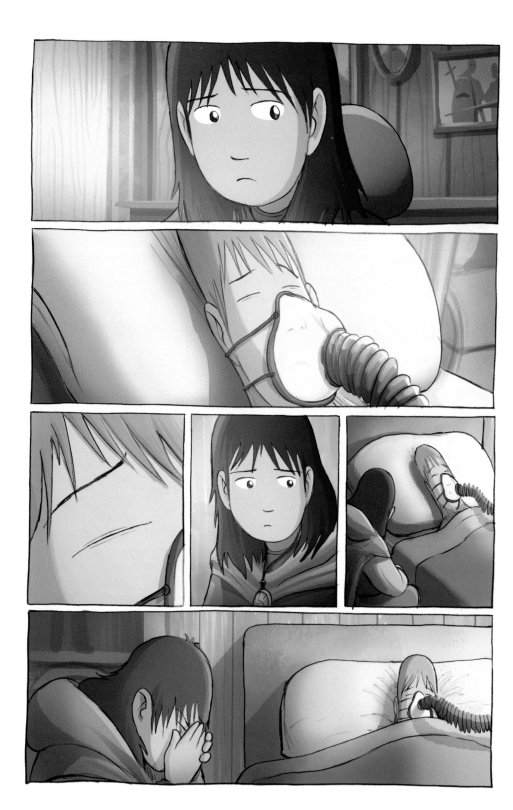

SNIF

HMM.

WHAT IS IT, MORRIE?

IT APPEARS YOUR MOTHER'S CONDITION IS WORSE.

THE POISON IS GROWING EVEN STRONGER.

CAN'T WE DO ANYTHING TO SLOW IT DOWN?

I'VE TRIED EVERYTHING.

BUT THE POISON IS TOO POWERFUL FOR THE MEDICINES WE HAVE HERE.

I JUST HOPE THE DOCTORS IN KANALIS HAVE SOMETHING.

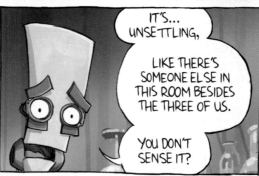

HWEEEEE

THEY'RE COMING.

WHO IS?

WE SHOULD HAVE DESTROYED THE ELF PRINCE WHEN WE HAD THE CHANCE.

NOW THEY WILL STOP AT NOTHING TO KILL YOU.

WHY WOULD THEY WANT TO KILL ME?

BY NOT JOINING THEM, YOU HAVE BECOME THEIR SWORN ENEMY. YOU ARE SIMPLY TOO POWERFUL FOR THEM TO LEAVE YOU ALONE.

YOU MUST PREPARE FOR BATTLE.

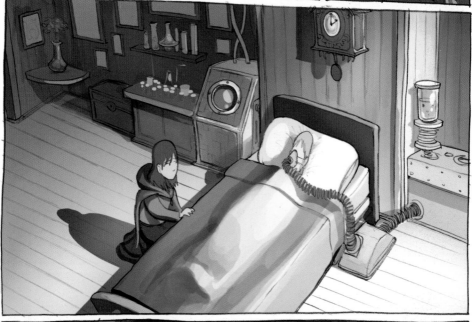

21

SHOULD WE ATTACK THEM NOW, SIR?

NOT YET.

HAVE SOMEONE FOLLOW THEM.

WE WILL NEED TO SEPARATE THEM FROM THEIR HOUSE IN ORDER TO TAKE IT OVER.

NOW WATCH CAREFULLY, TRELLIS.

I'M GOING TO SHOW YOU HOW TO EARN YOUR FATHER'S TRUST.

NOW, BEFORE WE STEP OUTSIDE, I SHOULD PROBABLY LET YOU KNOW THAT MANY OF THE CITIZENS HERE MIGHT LOOK QUITE A BIT... DIFFERENT.

DIFFERENT? WHAT DO YOU MEAN, MISKIT?

JUST DON'T STARE AT THEM.

FWOOOOSH!

27

WELCOME TO KANALIS.

PLEASE HAVE YOUR PASSPORTS READY, AND PREPARE FOR BOARDING AND INSPECTION.

DO ALL OF THE PEOPLE OF KANALIS LOOK LIKE HIM?

NO.

KANALIS IS A PORT TOWN, SO PEOPLE FROM ALL WALKS OF LIFE END UP HERE.

IT IS SAID THAT EVERYONE IN ALLEDIA FINDS THEIR WAY HERE EVENTUALLY.

SO LET'S HOPE THAT PROVES TRUE WITH THE LAND'S FINEST DOCTORS.

WE'RE GOING TO NEED A VERY GOOD ONE.

MANY OF THESE TOWNSFOLK ARE VERY SLOWLY BEING ALTERED BY AN ANCIENT CURSE.

IT IS WHAT GIVES THEM THE APPEARANCE OF ANIMALS.

BUT THAT'S TERRIBLE!

I DON'T BELIEVE THEY SEE IT AS ANYTHING QUITE SO NEGATIVE.

THIS CURSE HAS AFFECTED THEM FOR SO MANY YEARS THAT THE NEW GENERATIONS SEE IT AS SIMPLY A FACT OF LIFE.

IS IT CONTAGIOUS?

THAT'S A GOOD QUESTION!

I HAVE THEM IN MY SIGHTS, SIR.

GOOD.

STRIKE SWIFTLY AND SILENTLY.

THE CHILDREN ARE PRIORITY ONE.

YES, SIR.

THEY WON'T EVEN KNOW WHAT HIT THEM.

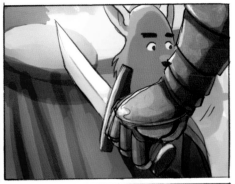

SHH.

MAYBE WE SHOULD ASK SOMEONE, MISKIT.

DO NOT WORRY, MISS EMILY.

I KNOW MY WAY AROUND HERE.

WHAT ARE THOSE PEOPLE WAITING FOR?

THEY'RE IN LINE FOR THE SOUP KITCHEN.

HMM.

I DON'T REMEMBER SEEING SO MANY HUNGRY BEFORE.

SHUT HIM UP!!

WAHH!

PLEASE, SIR.

YOU'RE SCARING HIM!

WAHH!

IF YOU DON'T SHUT HIM UP, YOU'RE GOING TO HAVE ONE LESS MOUTH TO FEED!!!

LEAVE THEM ALONE.

WAAAH!

HEY!

MIND YOUR OWN BUSINESS!

HEY, ALEX, BE STRONG.

BE STRONG AND QUIET FOR YOUR MOMMY, OKAY?

NOD.

IT JUST TAKES A LITTLE PATIENCE.

GRRR.

POW!!!

OOF!

ERRRR...

I TOLD YOU TO MIND YOUR OWN BUSINESS.

NNNGH.

37

ARACHNOPODS ARE HIGHLY TOXIC.

MOST CASES RESULT IN DEATH.

SHE'S LUCKY TO STILL BE ALIVE!

CAN YOU HELP HER?

ONLY THE FRUIT OF A GADOBA TREE CAN FIGHT THE VENOM AND CURE HER.

DO YOU KNOW WHERE I CAN FIND ONE?

THE LAST REMAINING TREES STAND AT THE PEAK OF DEMON'S HEAD MOUNTAIN...

BUT EVEN THE ELVES WON'T GO THERE.

MANY ELVES SET OUT IN SEARCH OF THE HEALING GADOBA FRUITS. THE ELF KING WOULD ORDER HIS MEN TO REGULARLY CLIMB TO THE SUMMIT. AND OF THE HUNDREDS SENT --

-- NONE HAVE RETURNED.

I CAN'T LET YOU GO THERE IN GOOD CONSCIENCE.

IT'S FAR TOO DANGEROUS.

HEY, GUYS?

I DON'T THINK GOING THERE'S A GOOD IDEA.

I'M HERE FOR ONLY ONE REASON, AND THAT'S TO GET MY FAMILY HOME SAFE.

IF THAT MEANS WE HAVE TO CLIMB A MOUNTAIN, THEN THAT'S WHAT WE'RE GOING TO DO.

IS THAT REALLY THE ONLY REASON?

41

RING RING! ♪♪

HELLO?

WE'VE GOT A PROBLEM.

THE ELVES ARE ABOUT TO STORM THE HOUSE.

THEODORE, TELL EVERYONE TO GET READY.

IS EVERYONE HERE?

I'M GOING TO DO A COMPLETE SHUTDOWN SO THE ELVES CAN'T GET ANY INFORMATION.

BUT THAT MEANS WE'LL BE FULLY OUT OF COMMISSION, UNDERSTAND?

IT'LL BE UP TO YOU TO TURN US BACK ON.

AND YOU BETTER GET HERE BEFORE THEY TURN US INTO SCRAP METAL!

I'M COUNTIN' ON YOU, BUDDY!

READY?

CLICK!

BZAK!

SZT!

LOOK,

YOU'RE GOING TO NEED MY HELP.

WHETHER YOU LIKE IT OR NOT.

IS THERE AN UNDERGROUND EXIT HERE?

WE HAVE AN EMERGENCY RAIL SYSTEM THAT RUNS THROUGH THE CITY'S ABANDONED MINE SHAFTS.

IT LEADS TO A SAFE HOUSE.

SEND ALL YOUR PATIENTS AND STAFF TO THE ESCAPE ROUTE NOW.

EVERYONE?

WAIT, WHY ARE WE TAKING THE PATIENTS WITH US?

BECAUSE THE ELVES ARE ALREADY HERE.

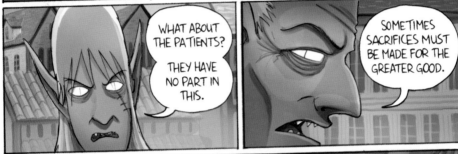

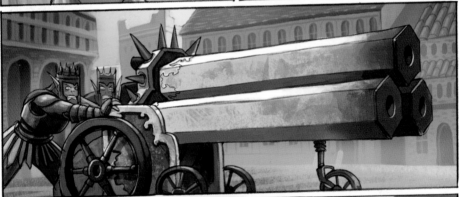

CHOOM!!!

WHAT WAS THAT?

WE HAVE TO LEAVE.

NOW.

EVERYONE, THIS WAY!

DOWNSTAIRS, QUICKLY!

WATCH YOUR STEP!

THIS WAY.

THE COAST IS CLEAR.

THE ELVES TOOK OVER THE STREETS.

WHAT DO WE DO NOW?

WE TAKE THE HIGH ROAD.

WHAT ARE YOU WAITING FOR?

ARE YOU KIDDING?!

WE CAN'T DO THAT!

THIS IS WHY YOU SHOULDN'T HAVE TAGGED ALONG!

YOU CAN'T, BUT SHE CAN.

I DON'T KNOW HOW.

SHE DOESN'T KNOW HOW!!

YES SHE DOES.

NOW STOP FOOLING AROUND DOWN THERE OR YOU'RE GOING TO GET US KILLED!

GET ON MY BACK.

DON'T LET HIM BULLY YOU.

C'MON.

YOU SURE ABOUT THIS, EMILY?

VERY GOOD!

NOW TRY AND KEEP UP WITH ME!

HE HAS TO BE JOKING.

THERE'S NO SIGN OF THEM ANYWHERE, SIR.

THEN YOU'RE NOT LOOKING HARD ENOUGH.

IS THIS WHAT YOU WANTED TO SHOW ME?

PATIENCE, WE ARE ONLY GETTING WARMED UP.

BEEP BEEP!

WHAT IS IT?

WE'VE SPOTTED THEM, SIR.

THEY'RE UP ON THE ROOFTOPS.

58

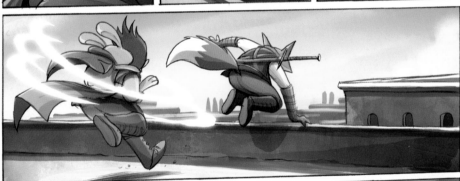

DESTROY
THEM.

LOOK OUT,
GUYS!

WE'VE GOT
COMPANY!

EMILY! LOOK OUT!

SZRAK!!!

KRRRK
KEK

LEON NEEDS MY HELL!

I CAN USE THE STONE...

BUT WHAT IF YOU CAN'T CONTROL IT?

WHAT IF YOU HIT LEON BY ACCIDENT?

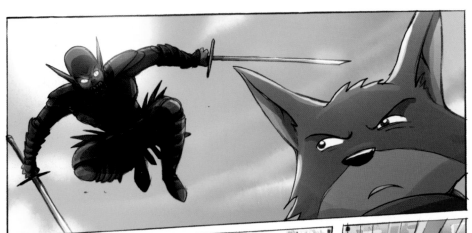

CLASP!

ERRGH!

AGH!

SO EASY, ISN'T IT?

SO EASY TO HAVE SO MUCH POWER.

GET OUT...

OF...

...MY HEAD!

EMILY!

UNH!

OOF!!

EMILY!

EMILY, GET UP!

UNNH...

GET IT OFF OF ME!!!

WHY CAN'T I GET THIS STUPID THING OFF?!

IT IS YOUR CURSE.

I'M SORRY IT HAS COME DOWN TO YOU, EMILY,

BUT IT IS YOUR CHOSEN PATH.

YOU HAVE YET TO UNDERSTAND THE EXTENT OF YOUR POWER,

BUT WHEN YOU DO, AND YOU LEARN TO CONTROL IT, I HAVE FAITH THAT YOU WILL TURN THIS CURSE INTO A BLESSING FOR YOU AND ALLEDIA.

MILTON, PLEASE SHOW THIS GENTLEMAN WHERE TO TAKE THE PATIENT.

YES, BALAN.

YOU SAID THIS PLACE WAS THE HEADQUARTERS. BUT FOR WHAT?

LET ME SHOW YOU.

WELCOME.

TO THE RESISTANCE.

WE'VE GATHERED WARRIORS THE WORLD OVER TO AID IN OUR FIGHT AGAINST THE ELVES.

THEY ARE ALLEDIA'S LAST, BEST HOPE.

OH MY GOSH.

IT'S HIM!

WHOA!

OH BOY, OH BOY.

SKITTER SKITTER

IT IS AN INCREDIBLE HONOR TO MEET YOU, SIR.

SIR? WHY ARE THEY CALLING ME THAT?

YOU'LL FIND OUT SOON ENOUGH.

COME. THERE'S SOMEONE WAITING TO MEET YOU.

HE'S AN OLD FRIEND OF YOUR GREAT-GRAND-FATHER SILAS.

AND ONE OF THE FIRST MEMBERS OF THE RESISTANCE.

HIS NAME IS FATHER ADLER.

IS HE A PRIEST?

NOT QUITE.

PLEASE, HAVE A SEAT.

DO YOU KNOW WHY YOU'RE HERE?

WE'RE HERE TO SAVE MY MOM'S LIFE.

OH, BUT YOU WILL DO MUCH MORE THAN THAT.

SO YOU CAN REALLY SEE THE FUTURE?

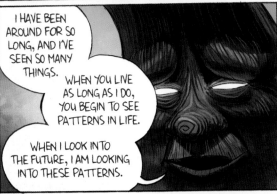

I HAVE BEEN AROUND FOR SO LONG, AND I'VE SEEN SO MANY THINGS.

WHEN YOU LIVE AS LONG AS I DO, YOU BEGIN TO SEE PATTERNS IN LIFE.

WHEN I LOOK INTO THE FUTURE, I AM LOOKING INTO THESE PATTERNS.

YOU CREATURES ARE NOT AS COMPLEX AS YOU MAKE YOURSELVES OUT TO BE.

IF YOU REALLY CAN SEE INTO THE FUTURE, THEN PLEASE TELL ME...

WILL MY SISTER BE OKAY?

IF THERE IS ONLY BAD NEWS TO TELL, DO YOU STILL WISH TO HEAR IT?

IT MIGHT BE BETTER TO SIMPLY HOPE FOR THE BEST.

I NEED TO KNOW THE TRUTH.

WILL SHE BE OKAY?

I SEE THE IMAGE OF YOUR SISTER ARRIVING AT THE SUMMIT OF DEMON'S HEAD MOUNTAIN.

THERE SHE WILL MEET MY BROTHERS, AND SHE WILL ATTEMPT TO PICK THE FRUIT THAT WILL CURE YOUR MOTHER.

THE IMAGES THAT FOLLOW ARE MUCH LESS CLEAR.

BUT ONE PICTURE APPEARS VIVIDLY.

IT IS THE IMAGE OF YOUR SISTER FALLING OFF OF A CLIFF.

SHE IS UNCONSCIOUS, AND DEATH AWAITS HER BELOW.

NO.

MORRIE! WE HAVE TO LEAVE!

NOW!

WAIT! YOU'RE SUPPOSED TO HEAR ABOUT YOUR FUTURE!

PARDON THE INTERRUPTION, SIR, BUT IT SOUNDS LIKE YOU COULD USE AN ARMY.

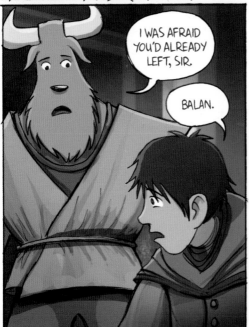

I WAS AFRAID YOU'D ALREADY LEFT, SIR.

BALAN.

NOT YOU, TOO! WHY IS EVERYONE CALLING ME 'SIR'?

BECAUSE YOU ARE THIS ARMY'S COMMANDER.

C-COMMANDER?

85

OTHERWISE, YOU WILL POSE A GREATER THREAT TO OUR SAFETY THAN EVEN OUR ENEMIES.

BUT HER MOTHER GROWS WORSE BY THE HOUR.

WE DON'T HAVE TIME!

THEN WE MUST WORK SWIFTLY.

EMILY, YOU WILL NEED TO CHOOSE A WEAPON.

I CAN OFFER YOU MY SWORD.

WHY DO I NEED A WEAPON?

IT WILL ALLOW YOU TO HARNESS YOUR POWER AND FOCUS YOUR ENERGY.

KEEP YOUR SWORD.

HOW ABOUT THIS WALKING STICK?

VERY WELL.

IT SHOULD BE ADEQUATE FOR OUR PURPOSES.

NOW FOLLOW ME.

SHHK...

LEON.

WHY ARE YOU DOING THIS?

WHY ARE YOU HELPING US?

BECAUSE IN THE END, IT WILL BE YOU HELPING ALL OF US.

I'M ONLY HERE TO SHOW YOU THE WAY.

I DON'T UNDERSTAND.

HOW MUCH DID SILAS TELL YOU ABOUT HIS LIFE'S WORK?

I-I DIDN'T GET A CHANCE TO SPEAK WITH HIM ABOUT IT BEFORE HE PASSED AWAY.

WELL, WHAT HE WOULD HAVE TOLD YOU IS THAT THERE IS A GROUP OF PEOPLE IN ALLEDIA FIGHTING AGAINST THE ELF KING'S TERRIBLE RULE.

SILAS WAS ONE OF THESE PEOPLE.

AND NOW YOU HAVE TAKEN HIS PLACE.

BUT ALL I WANT TO DO IS FIND A CURE FOR MY MOM AND GET MY FAMILY BACK HOME SAFELY.

AND I WILL HELP YOU DO THAT,

BUT THE TRUTH IS THAT YOU HAVE AN EVEN GREATER MISSION AHEAD OF YOU.

YOU MUST UNDERSTAND THAT IF WE DO NOT STOP THE ELF KING, YOUR MOTHER WILL NOT BE THE ONLY ONE TO DIE.

IF WE FAIL, WE WILL ALL PERISH.

BUT WHY ME?

IT'S IN YOUR BLOOD, EMILY.

BUT MY MOM, AND HER FATHER --

THEY'RE DESCENDANTS OF SILAS, TOO.

WHY DIDN'T THEY WEAR THE STONE?

BECAUSE SILAS CHOSE TO LEAVE THEM IN THE DARK.

HE KEPT THEM UNAWARE OF THEIR DUTY AS HEIRS TO THE STONE, AND LEFT THEM TO LEAD WHAT HE FELT WAS A NORMAL LIFE.

WHAT HE FAILED TO REALIZE IS THAT BY KEEPING THEM FROM THEIR FATE,

HE HAS PASSED THEIR BURDEN DOWN TO YOU.

HOW CAN YOU SAY HE FAILED?

HE ONLY DID WHAT HE THOUGHT WAS BEST FOR HIS FAMILY.

EVEN WITH YOUR MOTHER'S LIFE ON THE LINE, AND THE LIVES OF HER CHILDREN THREATENED,

YOU WOULD SAY HE DID NOT FAIL?

HAD SILAS CHOSEN TO DO WHAT IS RIGHT FOR ALL OF US, HE COULD HAVE SPARED YOU FROM THIS CURSE.

OR MY MOM COULD HAVE DIED TRYING.

NOT EVERYBODY WANTS TO BE A HERO, LEON.

BUT THEY SHOULD.

NOW LOOK HERE, MISTER REDBEARD.

I KNOW YOU'RE SOME KIND OF GREAT WARRIOR, BUT SILAS LEFT NO MENTION OF YOU.

HE DID, HOWEVER, LEAVE ME TO LOOK AFTER MY MASTER, EMILY.

NOW IF YOU'LL KINDLY SHOW US THE WAY UP THE MOUNTAIN, WE CAN BE ON OUR WAY.

FINE.

IF THAT IS ALL YOU CARE ABOUT, THEN FOLLOW ME.

SEE?

YOU JUST HAVE TO ASK NICELY.

WHAT IS THAT?

IT IS THE ENTRANCE TO THE ONLY KNOWN PASSAGEWAY UP DEMON'S HEAD MOUNTAIN.

YES, BUT WHAT IS THAT BLOCKING THE WAY?

TWENTY TONS OF EXPLOSIVES.

IF ANYONE WERE TO TRY AND IGNITE IT, THE EXPLOSION WOULD DESTROY THE ENTRANCE.

AND THE INTRUDERS.

IT IS MEANT TO BE A SAFEGUARD TO KEEP PEOPLE AWAY FROM THIS PLACE.

SZRAK!

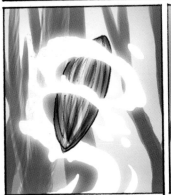

FWOOM!

TOK!

AGAIN.

SZRAK!

FWOOM!!!

BUT WITH MISKIT, IT'S DIFFERENT.

HOW SO?

I-I DON'T KNOW. IT JUST IS.

AND WHY DO YOU THINK THAT IS?

BECAUSE! I DON'T WANT TO HURT HIM, I WANT TO PROTECT HIM.

HE'S A LIVING THING.

WELL, SO IS THIS SEED. NOW PROTECT IT.

IT'S NOT THE SAME.

BUT IT IS.

SOON, YOU'LL COME TO UNDERSTAND THAT EVERYTHING HAS A LIFE FORCE...

SOME LIVES ARE EASY TO DETECT.

KSHING!

BUT TO FIND OTHERS, YOU HAVE TO LOOK BENEATH THE SURFACE.

LISTEN FOR YOUR STAFF'S LIFE FORCE AND FOCUS YOUR ENERGY ON IT.

TREAT IT LIKE A PART OF YOU.

NOW TRY PICKING UP THE SEED.

TREAT IT THE SAME WAY.

FOCUS.

WELL DONE.

LET'S TRY SOMETHING A LITTLE BIGGER.

CATCH!

WELCOME BACK, YOUNG MASTER.

I WAS BEGINNING TO THINK YOU WERE UPSET WITH ME.

FEEL THAT POWER, YOUNG MASTER.

WITH IT, WE CAN ACCOMPLISH ANYTHING.

DOOM!

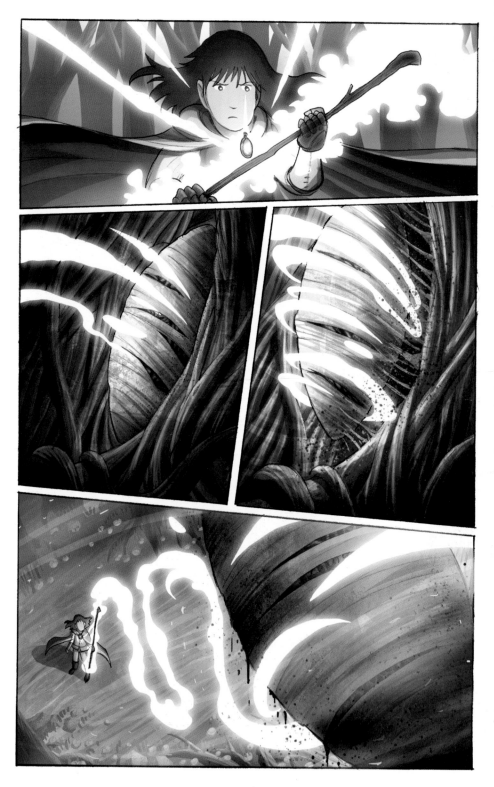

EMILY?

YOU DON'T NEED THEM, MASTER.

WE CAN DO THIS ON OUR OWN.

ARE YOU OKAY?

THEY'LL ONLY SLOW US DOWN AND MAKE US WEAKER.

LEAVE THEM BEHIND.

THIS ROAD BELONGS TO US.

YOU'RE GROWING IN STRENGTH.

AND SO IS THE STONE.

THE MORE POWERFUL THE AMULET BECOMES, THE MORE DIFFICULT IT WILL BE TO CONTROL.

AND WHAT HAPPENS IF I LOSE CONTROL?

THEN WE WOULD BE IN A WHOLE HEAP OF TROUBLE.

BUT IT WON'T HAPPEN.

HOW DO YOU KNOW?

BECAUSE I BELIEVE THE GADOBA TREES WERE RIGHT ABOUT YOU.

THE GADOBA TREES?

YOU CAN SPEAK TO THEM?

OF COURSE.

AND I IMAGINE THEY LOOK FORWARD TO SPEAKING WITH YOU, TOO.

NOW, FOLLOW ME.

WE DON'T HAVE TIME TO LOSE.

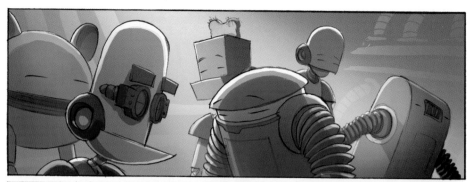

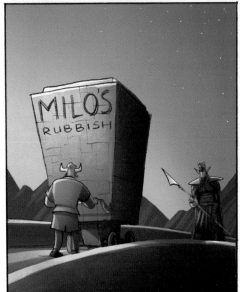

GAK!

OH, THAT'S RIGHT.

ELVES CAN'T STAND THE SMELL OF FISH, CAN THEY?

THE LAST PICKUP WAS THE MARINA. SORRY.

HMM. I SUPPOSE THAT'S WHY WE GET TO HAVE THESE JOBS.

LUCKY US.

GO! JUST HURRY AND GO!!

GAK!

HACK! COUGH!

HEH, HEH.

FSHT!

OKAY, BOYS, YOU'RE UP.

HMM.

YOU FIRST.

SHLP! SHLP!

UGH!

TRASH

OOF!

WE NEED TO GET TO THE ATTIC.

SPAK!

SZT! SZT!

SZRAK!

WELCOME BACK, COGSLEY.

THANKS, CHIEF.

NOW HELP ME GET US OUT OF HERE.

BOOT SEQUENCE INITIATED.

WE SHOULD BE UP AND RUNNING IN THIRTY MINUTES.

COGSLEY, DO YOU BELIEVE IN PREMONITIONS?

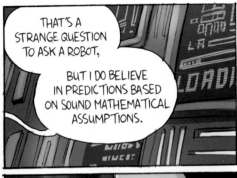

THAT'S A STRANGE QUESTION TO ASK A ROBOT,

BUT I DO BELIEVE IN PREDICTIONS BASED ON SOUND MATHEMATICAL ASSUMPTIONS.

IF THE "PREMONITIONS" WERE BASED ON SUCH MATH, I WOULD BELIEVE THEM.

THEN LET'S HOPE TREES ARE BAD AT MATH.

PSHT!

YOU'RE GOING TO KILL YOURSELF.

WE BETTER REST HERE FOR NOW.

YOU NEVER ANSWERED MY QUESTION, LEON.

WHAT HAPPENS TO A STONEKEEPER WHEN THEY LOSE CONTROL OF THE STONE?

THEY...
...CHANGE.

CHANGE?

THIRTY YEARS AGO, A GROUP OF FOUR YOUNG STONEKEEPERS LOST CONTROL OF THEIR POWERS...

THE RESISTANCE WAS ABLE TO DESTROY THESE POWER-HUNGRY ROGUE STONEKEEPERS.

EXCEPT FOR ONE.

HE USED TO BE A QUIET BOY FROM A SMALL ELF VILLAGE, BUT AFTER HIS TRANSFORMATION, HE WAS NEVER THE SAME.

THE ELDERS WERE ABLE TO SEPARATE HIM FROM HIS STONE, AND DESPITE HIS REQUESTS TO BE EXECUTED, THEY LOCKED HIM UP IN AN ATTEMPT TO CURE HIM OF ITS CURSE.

BUT WHEN HE TALKED, HE SPOKE ONLY OF HIS DESIRE FOR POWER, AND WARNED OF DARK DAYS TO COME.

HE TOLD THEM THAT THEY WOULD REGRET HAVING KEPT HIM ALIVE,

AND THAT HE WOULD SHOW THEM WHY.

SO THAT BOY WAS THE ELF KING.

YES.

IS THAT WHY YOU'RE DOING THIS? BECAUSE HE KILLED YOUR FATHER?

I AM NOT MOTIVATED BY VENGEANCE. I DO THIS TO HONOR HIM.

THESE STONES ARE WHAT KILLED YOUR FATHER.

SO HOW CAN YOU TRUST ME?

MY MISSION HAS ALWAYS BEEN TO DESTROY THE ELF KING.

AND YOU'RE THE BEST HOPE I HAVE FOR SEEING THAT HAPPEN.

WHAT ARE YOU HIDING, TRELLIS?

HIDING?

I CAN SENSE YOUR HESITATION.

THE AIR AROUND YOU IS AS THICK AS BLOOD.

THE GADOBA FOREST SHOULD BE AROUND HERE SOMEWHERE.

I DON'T SEE ANYTHING.

THE FOG IS TOO THICK.

THAT'S STRANGE.

SHOULDN'T THOSE TREES BE RIGHT --

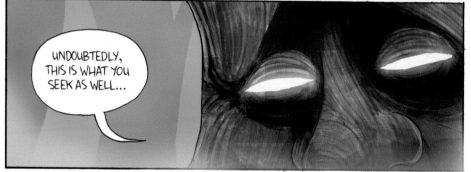

I--

BROTHER MALKEN!

I SENSE SOMETHING DIFFERENT ABOUT THIS ONE.

DON'T YOU?

YES... YES...

DIFFERENT INDEED.

WHY DID ALL THESE PEOPLE DIE?

BECAUSE THEY PICKED THE WRONG FRUIT, OF COURSE.

FOR EVERY ONE FRUIT THAT GIVES LIFE, THERE ARE A HUNDRED THAT TAKE IT AWAY.

VERY FEW SUCCEED IN FINDING THEIR PRIZE.

LEON REDBEARD.

IT HAS BEEN A LONG TIME, MY FRIEND.

I PROMISED THAT I WOULD RETURN.

YES.

AND NOW YOU BELIEVE THIS GIRL TO BE THE ONE WE'RE LOOKING FOR?

I AM CERTAIN OF IT.

VERY WELL.

SHOW US.

EMILY, CHOOSE A FRUIT, AND EAT IT.

BUT HOW DO I CHOOSE THE RIGHT ONE?

JUST REMEMBER WHAT I TOLD YOU.

EVERYTHING HAS A LIFE FORCE.

THIS IS THE ONE.

EMILY, WAIT!

SQUISH!!

UGH!

EMILY!

I'M FINE.

IT JUST TASTES TERRIBLE.

LEON IS RIGHT.

YOU DO HAVE THE GIFT.

THERE IS MORE WHERE THAT CAME FROM.

PLEASE FEEL FREE TO HARVEST THEM.

LEON, IS THIS ENOUGH TO CURE MY MOTHER?

YES.

139

THEN THIS IS ALL WE NEED.

THANK YOU FOR YOUR HELP.

NO.

THANK YOU, YOUNG STONEKEEPER.

AND GOOD LUCK.

WHAT ARE YOU DOING?

WE SHOULD TAKE AS MANY AS WE CAN!

WHAT IF WE LOSE THAT ONE?

AND JUST IMAGINE WHAT WE COULD DO WITH MORE!

IF WE TAKE MORE THAN WE NEED, WE'RE BOUND TO CAUSE MORE TROUBLE.

I TOLD YOU I'M HERE TO SAVE MY MOM.

THAT'S IT.

BUT...

BUT...

AT LEAST GET A FRESH ONE!

SH!

WHAT IS IT?

I SAW SOMETHING MOVING OUT THERE.

WE NEED TO LEAVE NOW.

I'M SORRY, FATHER MALKEN.

IT'S LIKELY THAT ELVES ARE ON OUR TRAIL.

WE WERE CARELESS.

DO NOT WORRY ABOUT US, LEON.

LEAVE QUICKLY AND KEEP THE STONEKEEPER SAFE.

IT WILL BE UP TO YOU TO SEE THAT SHE REACHES HER FULL POTENTIAL.

AND BE CAREFUL --

REGARDLESS, I CANNOT LET SUCH CRIMES GO UNPUNISHED,

NOW CAN I?

BURN THEM DOWN. ALL OF THEM.

YES, SIR.

BROTHER MALKEN, IS THIS THE END?

WE ARE NOT THE LAST OF THE GADOBA, BROTHER HENN.

SO LET US HOPE THIS IS ONLY A NEW BEGINNING.

HEY --

WE HAVE TO GO BACK.

NO.

THERE'S NOTHING WE CAN DO TO HELP.

THE ELVES ARE CLOSE, SO WE MUST HURRY.

LET'S GO.

EMILY,

DON'T YOU SEE THE TROUBLE YOU ARE CAUSING FOR OTHERS?

WE CAN END ALL OF THEIR SUFFERING NOW.

YOU CAN- NOT RELY ON THEM --

FOR THEIR SAKE.

YOU MUST TAKE MATTERS INTO YOUR OWN HANDS!

YOU AND I CAN DESTROY THE ELVES OURSELVES.

JUST LET THE STONE TAKE CONTROL.

NO.

I NEED TO BELIEVE IN MY FRIENDS AND FAMILY.

WHY?

BECAUSE YOU SEE THAT THEY ARE VALUABLE IN YOUR QUEST FOR POWER?

NO.

I NEED TO BELIEVE IN THEM --

BECAUSE THEY BELIEVE IN ME.

AND HOW WILL YOU FEEL WHEN THEY ALL DIE FOR YOU?

THAT WON'T HAPPEN.

HOW CAN YOU BE SO SURE?

BECAUSE I WON'T LET IT HAPPEN.

SNAP!

DID YOU HEAR THAT?

REMEMBER, RETAIN CONTROL OF YOUR POWER.

THE MORE ENERGY YOU USE, THE STRONGER THE STONE BECOMES.

YOU MUST NOT LET IT TAKE OVER.

I WON'T.

KILL THEM.

HWEEEEH!

DOOM!

HE IS MUCH TOO POWERFUL.

IN KNOWLEDGE AND SKILL YOU ARE OUTMATCHED.

THERE IS ONLY ONE WAY FOR YOU TO DEFEAT HIM.

YOU MUST GIVE CONTROL TO THE STONE.

AAAAH!

KRAK!

EMILY, GET UP! GET UP NOW!

I'M THE ONE IN CONTROL!

ACCEPT THE STONE'S FULL POWER BEFORE IT'S TOO LATE!

AND YOU WILL DIE HOLDING ON TO IT! LET THE STONE TAKE OVER AND MAKE YOUR TRANSFORMATION COMPLETE!

URK!

AAH!

WHAP!!

SHIVER SHIVER

SO THIS IS THE STONEKEEPER WHO WOULD DESTROY THE KING.

HOW IS IT POSSIBLE THAT YOU COULD POSE SUCH A GREAT THREAT?

GOOD-BYE, YOUNG STONEKEEPER.

I WOULD HAVE PREFERRED A SPIRITED BATTLE, BUT AN EXECUTION WILL DO.

SHIVER SHIVER

AGH!

SKRAK!!

LITTLE WORM,

WHAT DO YOU THINK YOU'RE DOING?!

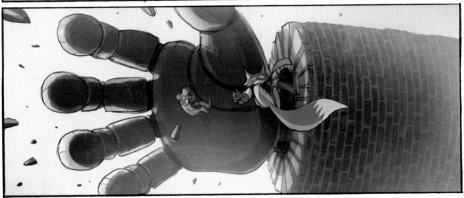

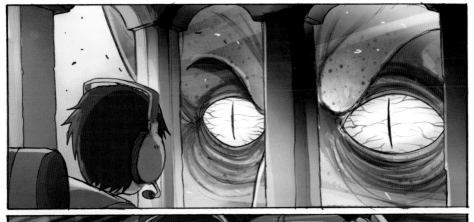

183

185

NO.

I CAN DEFEAT IT WITHOUT LOSING CONTROL.

BUT HOW CAN YOU FIGHT SUCH A MONSTER WITHOUT BECOMING ONE YOURSELF?

BY NOT FIGHTING ALONE.

NAVIN...

EM!

GET BACK IN THE DRIVER'S SEAT.

I'M GOING TO NEED YOUR HELP.

BUT... THE HOUSE IS DESTROYED.

WHAT DO YOU INTEND TO DO?

IT'S LIKE YOU SAID, LEON.

EVERYTHING HAS A LIFE FORCE.

WHAT'S HAPPENING NOW?

I DON'T KNOW, BUT STAY IN THAT SEAT.

SIZZLE

SZRAK!

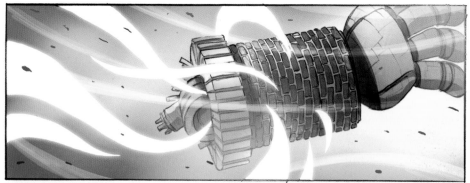

WELL, LOOK AT THAT.

ALL SYSTEMS ARE BACK ONLINE.

I'M GOING TO NEED SOME OF THE AUXILIARY POWER TO PUSH US BACK UP.

YOU READY?

PUNCH IT, COGSLEY!

KSHT!

MORE POWER, EM!!!

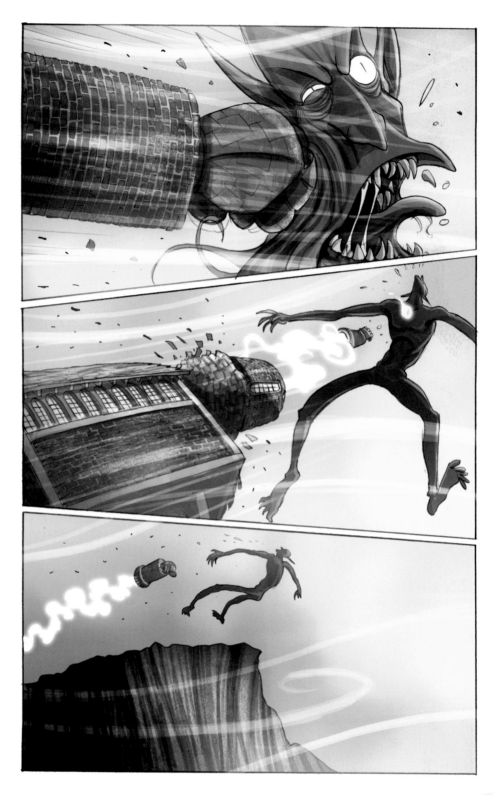

WE DID IT!!!

-SZT!

SPRAK!

WE'RE LOSING POWER!

EM?

EM!!

UNNHN...

SIZZLE SIZZLE!

IF THIS IS A DREAM, I DON'T WANT TO WAKE UP.

THIS ISN'T A DREAM, SWEETIE.

EVERYTHING'S GOING TO BE ALL RIGHT.

WE'RE GOING HOME NOW.

NO, MOM.

ONLY YOU AND NAVIN ARE GOING HOME.

I HAVE TO STAY HERE.

EVEN IF I TRIED TO LEAVE,

I THINK SOMETHING WOULD STOP ME.

THEN I'LL STAY HERE UNTIL WE CAN ALL GO HOME TOGETHER.

BUT YOU CAN'T STAY HERE!

EM!

NAVIN!

YOU DID GOOD.

YOU BOTH PERFORMED ADMIRABLY.

YOUR MOTHER SHOULD BE VERY PROUD.

SO WE WON?

FOR NOW.

BUT THIS IS ONLY THE BEGINNING.

THE ELVES WILL NOW COME AFTER US WITH THE FULL STRENGTH OF THEIR ARMY.

WE'LL BE READY.

YES, BUT IN ORDER TO BE READY, WE WILL NEED TO WORK HARD AND PREPARE.

YOUR TRAINING BEGINS TOMORROW, SO GET SOME REST.

LOOKS LIKE YOU ALL HAVE SOME CATCHING UP TO DO.

I'LL LEAVE YOU BE.

THANK YOU, LEON.

FOR EVERYTHING.

GET SOME REST.

HE SEEMS LIKE A REALLY NICE --

-- ANIMAL PERSON.

WE JUST GOT THE MAIN ENGINE BACK ONLINE, CHIEF.

WE'LL BE OPERATIONAL BY THE END OF THE DAY.

NICE WORK, COGSLEY.

I'LL SEE YOU BACK IN THE CONTROL ROOM.

I GOTTA GO WASH MY HEAD.

MY GOODNESS, YOU GUYS SOUND SO... GROWN-UP.

I'M VERY IMPRESSED.

SO THIS IS OUR NEW HOME.

END OF BOOK TWO

WRITTEN AND DRAWN BY
KAZU KIBUISHI

COLORS AND BACKGROUNDS BY
KAZU KIBUISHI
AMY KIM KIBUISHI
ANTHONY GO WU
JASON CAFFOE

COLOR FLATTING ASSISTANCE BY
KEAN SOO
STUART LIVINGSTON
DENVER JACKSON
RYAN HOFFMANN
MICHAEL REGINA
TIM DURNING
CATHERINE YOO
ALAN BEADLE
PATRICK RACE
CAYLEIGH ALLEN
FELIX LIM